Living with DANGER

The Memoirs of a Bomb Disposal Officer

Captain H.W. Beckingham

First published 1997 by Countyvise Limited, 1 & 3 Grove Road, Rock Ferry, Birkenhead, Wirral, Merseyside L42 3XS in conjunction with the author Captain H.W. Beckingham

British Library Cataloguing in Publication Data.
A catalogue record for this book is available from the British Library.

ISBN 1 901231 03 8

The Author is indebted to the Royal Court, Guernsey, for their kind permission to reproduce a number of photographs from "Festung Guernsey".

Prologue

I consider myself extremely lucky to be one of the very few who served in Bomb Disposal from its inception in April 1940, and to have survived, when the average life expectancy for a Bomb Disposal Officer was ten weeks.

I lost many friends killed in dealing with Unexploded Bombs and Mines in the course of their duties dealing with these deadly devices. This book is my tribute to them.

Foreword

by Colonel B.S.T. Archer GC, OBE, ERD.

Henry Beckingham either kept a diary or has a prodigous memory, and is to be congratulated on compiling so many factual experiences over a long period serving in Bomb Disposal Units. Not many with that length of service survive to tell the tale.

It is not normally appreciated that Bomb Disposal Units are required to do their hazardous job, not only during war but for a long time after hostilities have ceased, therefore they spend more of their time "in action" than virtually any other member of the forces.

This book shows some of the varied activities which have to be carried out in Bomb Disposal. Being familiar with what went on in England I was especially interested in the work carried out in the Channel Islands and in particular in Guernsey.

20th June 1996.

The Author in 1946

Chapter One

In June 1988 my wife and I decided to take a holiday in Switzerland. The first town on our itinerary was to be Lugano. Having flown into Zurich airport we continued our journey by rail to our destination. On our arrival at Lugano railway station I noted how run down and forlorn the concourse looked, which prompted me to remark to my wife that this emptiness reminded me of the desolation I had encountered in the towns of St. Helier and St. Peter Port, when I had first landed in the Channel Islands in May 1945. Standing alongside me was a Guernsey man (Tony De La Mare) who having overheard our conversation asked if I had been part of Task Force 135 which had undertaken the liberation of the islands in May 1945. When I answered in the affirmative he asked if we could meet up after dinner that evening as he would very much like to hear from me how I had found the islands after five years of German occupation. He informed us that the Islands celebrated Liberation Day, as a National Holiday on the 9th May each year with parades, galas etc, and invited us to visit Guernsey as his guest in May 1989, so we could take part in their celebrations, and so from this chance meeting on a deserted station platform the idea for this book was born.

Forty four years had passed since I had first set foot on the island of Guernsey, I was surprised to find how life had changed, instead of the quiet idyllic countryside, so peaceful and tranquil, which I remembered, I was met on arrival in St Peter Port with a busy bustling town which had been overtaken by off-shore banks, tourists, and people seeking a tax haven. Traffic was very heavy due in part to the Hoteliers on the island offering free hire cars to their guests. The Island had been spoilt by the building of many hundreds of houses to cater for all the in-comers, banking staff etc. Large Marinas had been constructed in the harbour areas for the very affluent incomers to moor their yachts.

One day we drove out to Pleinmont Point on the Southern tip of the island which I remembered as the site of a German heavy gun battery, which had been protected by a series of minefields around its perimeter and also the site of one of the many reinforced concrete observation towers. As I stood looking out to sea I thought back over my life and the events that had brought me to the Channel Islands in 1945. Born in 1920 immediately after the First World War our lives as children was austere. The country was struggling to come to terms with itself after four years of war in which the flower of the countries manhood had been sacrificed on the battle fields of France. Generally the people were poor, there was much unemployment and those lucky enough to have a job received scant wages.

During my early years in the 1930s there were wars being fought around Europe and Africa. Italy had invaded Abyssinia in 1935, the Spanish Civil War had started in 1936. Italy had also invaded Albania in 1939 whilst Germany had annexed Austria and had also marched into Czechoslavakia. In short my years of growing up and my education had hardly been under ideal conditions. Born in Ludlow, Shropshire, and brought up in Eccles, Lancashire, whose one claim to fame was as the home of the "Original Eccles Cake".

I attended the local council school until I was eleven years of age, I then progressed to Eccles Grammar School, from where I went onto Salford Royal Technical College, which is now incorporated into Salford University to study structural engineering. In the Spring of 1938, I obtained my first employment as a trainee draughtsman with a firm of consulting engineers based in Manchester.

On the 22nd March 1939, German troops marched into the old German City of Memel, in Lithuania, forcing that state to sign a treaty conceding Memel be returned to the Fatherland. Poland recognising a parallel between Memel and the old German Port of Danzig announced that any attempt by Germany to alter the status of Danzig would lead to hostilities between the two countries. On the 25th May 1939, Britain entered into an non-aggression pact with Poland guaranteeing her borders.

The war clouds were now gathering fast over Europe.

The British Government introduced conscription on 14th April 1939, for men of 20 years of age and above. One had the option of joining the Territorial Army and serving four years on the basis of one annual 14 day camp per year plus a number of drill evenings at the local Drill Hall. The alternative was to wait to be called up and drafted into the Regular Army, where one would serve for a period of two years.

Whilst at Eccles Grammar School my two closest friends had on leaving school both gone into local government posts. The three of us decided to join the Territorial Army, but due to the introduction of conscription most technical arms had received a huge intake of volunteers. We had tried to enroll into the ROAC, RASC, and the Royal Engineers but without success. In the office where I worked there was a Major in the Territorial Army, incidently the Royal Engineers, to whom I related our problem. He suggested that if we presented ourselves at the Royal Engineers Drill Hall in Seymour Grove, Old Trafford, he would personally swear us in. Knowing the right people in the right place certainly paid off for us. On the 20th June 1939 we became "Sappers" in 201 Field Company RE, which formed part of the 42nd Division. In August the three of us went on holiday to Douglas, Isle of Man and had been back home a week when on Friday 1st September 1939 the Territorial Army

3

was mobilised, and we were ordered to report to our Units. On that date Germany had marched into Poland, and on the 2nd September an ultimatum was sent by the British Government to Hitler stating that unless Germany withdrew its troops immediately she must consider herself at war with Britain. On the 3rd September, Hitler received the ultimatum but chose to ignore it. I clearly remember the day, for as new recruits we had been marched into the Park adjacent to our drill hall and were receiving instruction on rifle drill when at 11.00 hours the announcement that Britain had declared war on Germany was issued.

201 Field Coy RE was to leave for France as part of the British Expedition Force shortly after mobilisation, but as I was only 19 years old I was transferred to 256 Field Coy RE which formed part of the 66th Division.

From September 1939 until March 1940 we were stationed at Stretford Grammar School and during this time we undertook basic weapon training and also field engineering works.

In March 1940 the Unit moved to Borwick Hall, Carnforth, Lancashire. It was rumoured that we were on our way to Norway via Scapa Flow, but the British Forces evacuated that country before we got there. It had been realised by the War Office that after an air-raid there could be a number of bombs dropped that had failed to explode either by design (delayed action) or due to a fault in the fusing system. These bombs would have a severe disorganising effect both on essential services and would impede the War effort. In April 1940 a number of Bomb Disposal Parties RE, were formed, these parties consisted of a Lance Corporal, one sapper and a driver. I was one of the first members of such a party. My party of three was despatched from Carnforth to Sheffield early in May, to be instructed on how to deal with Unexploded Bombs (UXBs). This course lasted for only two days. It had been assumed that after an air-raid any UXB would be found lying on the surface. (This assumption was to be soon proved wrong when the air-raids commenced on London.) The method of dealing with these bombs was to build a sandbagged wall around the bomb, leaving a small

4

access hole in the wall, so that one could crawl in and place a gun-cotton charge on the bomb casing. Corrugated iron sheeting was then placed across the top of the sandbagged wall and four layers of sandbags placed on top. Having placed the charge, one retired to a safe distance before detonating the bomb. Our party was issued with an Austin car which had been requisitioned and instructed to carry out a thorough reconnaissance of the City, so that in the event of an air raid we could go directly to any incident. Arrangements had also to be made to organise storage areas around the City where picks, shovels, sandbags, explosives etc, could be securely stored.

The "Three Musketeers" attached themselves to an RASC Unit which was stationed at Endcliffe Hall, Sheffield for "Pay and Rations" only.

During the summer of 1940 we spent a pleasant time touring Sheffield, and on many afternoons found ourselves at the YMCA in the City centre. In short we lanquished in idle obscurity waiting for some action. Two incidents occurred to relieve the boredom of our existence. In July we were called to Holmfirth, Nr. Wakefield, where on the Moors above the town a "Wellington" Bomber had jettisoned its bomb load before crashing. We collected explosives, detonators etc, from one of our store dumps and set off ready for action. On arrival in Holmfirth we were met by the local Constable and escorted to the site. We placed charges on the bombs which caused a huge explosion, which in turn caused considerable alarm over a wide area of West Yorkshire. Our second trip out found us making our way to Settle, North Yorkshire, again we were escorted by the local Constable onto the moors, here we found an unexploded "Ack Ack" shell which had been fired from a nearby gun-site.

In August 1940 we endeavoured to re-establish contact with our Unit (256 Field Coy RE) but to no avail. It appeared we had been forgotten and left to fend for ourselves. Our salvation came at the beginning of September, when a 2nd Lieutenant, Godsmark, arrived in Sheffield with 15 men from the Training Battalion at Chester, their designation was 35th Bomb Disposal Section RE. The strength of this unit was increased to 32 men shortly after its arrival in London on Monday 9th September 1940.

Chapter Two

On the 10th May 1940, the German armies launched their attacks against Holland, Belgium and France and by the 25th May the British Expedition Force had been squeezed into a small pocket around Dunkirk. A major sea evacuation was put into operation by the British Navy and during the nine days between 25th May and 4th June, 338,000 British and French troops were evacuated to England. This crushing defeat and the surrender of France on 22nd June 1940, led many members of the German High Command to believe that England would follow in the footsteps of France and sue for peace. When it was realised that England had no intentions of following this course of action plans were put into operation to carry out an invasion by sea (Operation Sealion). Before this could take place however the Luftwaffe had to drive the RAF from the skies over the English Channel and Southern England. Only when the RAF were put out of business could the Germans hope to mount their invasion. By August 10th the German Air Force stood ready to launch the major assault (Code-named "EAGLE"). Their initial attacks were on Radar installations and on the airfields from which the RAF fighter planes were operating, i.e. Lympne, Manston, Biggin Hill etc. Between the 24th August and the 6th September they made no less than 33 raids against these fighter stations.

The attacks on these airfields were doing well and was actually and steadily wearing down the RAF, but was not proving decisive. The German losses in planes and pilots was proving heavy and they had no wish to prolong this battle, their priority was the Invasion of Britain, which had been planned to take place on 21st September.

On Saturday 7th September the Germans changed the direction of their air offensive against Britain by making a devastating attack against the London Docks, this switch in tactics almost certainly saved the RAF. The strategy to attack the dock areas in the East End of London and totally destroy the Port of London was also to break the morale of the British people, the result, hopefully being that Britain would sue for peace.

In the afternoon 350 German bombers escorted by 600 fighters made for London, it was a beautiful summer's day with clear blue skies.

The Luftwaffe pilots had no difficulty in identifying their targets in the clear afternoon light. Now came an avalanche of bombs falling on the East End. Warehouses lining the River Thames from Woolwich to Tower Bridge were demolished or set ablaze.

Bombs were dropped on the Ford Motor Company Works at Dagenham and also on Beckton Gas Works. In the crowded dockland streets, large warehouses were set ablaze, and the dwellings in which the dockers lived were demolished under the weight of bombs, burying the occupants under the rubble. By 18.00 hours the raiders had returned to their bases in Northern France, but at 20.00 hours the second wave consisting of 247 bombers returned to the target area. The fires burning from the afternoon raid were to guide them to their targets. In this attack huge areas of timber stacked in the Surrey Commercial Docks were set alight. West Ham, Stepney, Poplar and Southwark suffered severe damage. The closely packed streets of East London were torn to pieces leaving piles of rubble where once stood neat little terraced houses. Hour upon hour the bombs rained down, demolishing many more

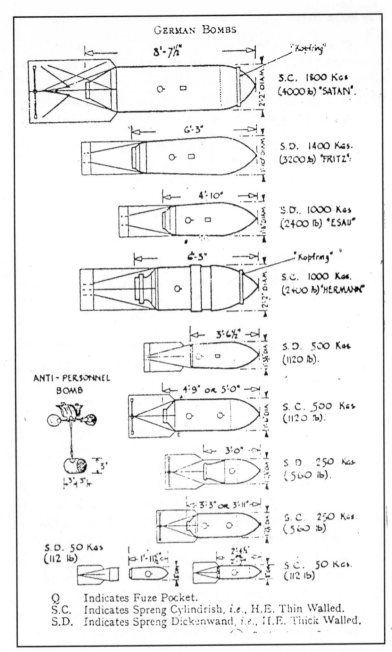

Main Categories of Bombs dropped on the United Kingdom.

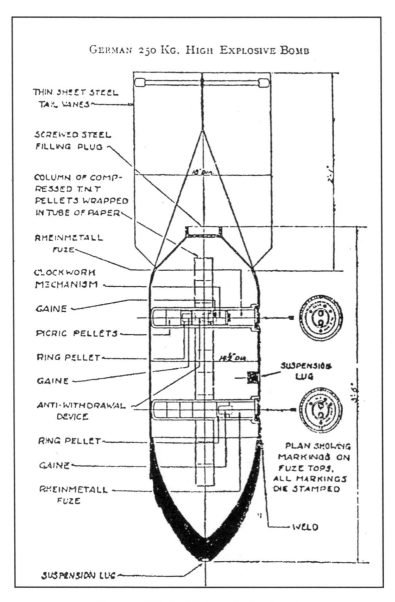

German 250 kg high explosive bomb.

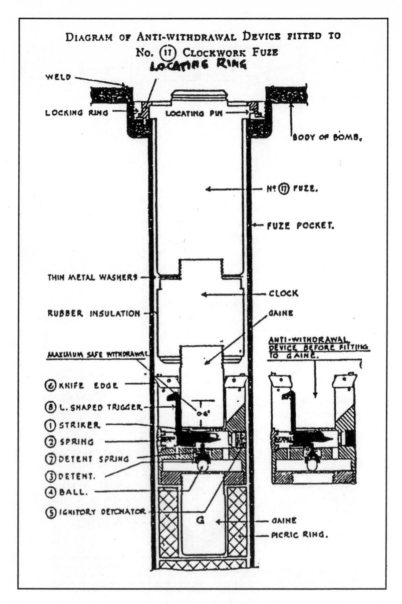

"*Fuze Pocket fitted with No (17) Fuze and ZUS 40*".

No. 35 Bomb Disposal Section RE.

Land Mine Casing, 1,000 kg Bomb (Herman) & 50 kg Bomb.

This picture shows a 50 kg, unexploded bomb being removed from an excavation in the Dockland area of Barking. (R. Matkin)

buildings and starting fresh fires. Against the glare of the flames parachute mines could be seen floating down which on landing would explode, the blast effect was such that a whole street would be demolished leaving nothing but dust and rubble. In this second raid 330 tonnes of High Explosive Bombs and 16,000 Incendiary Bombs were dropped.

On the 9th September, No.35 Bomb Disposal Section RE was ordered to London, where on arrival we moved to our billets at 41, Malford Grove, Wanstead, London E11. By this time the "Three Musketeers" had been taken onto the strength of the Section. We were now in the thick of the action, air-raids every night. There were also many during daylight hours. No.35 Bomb Disposal Section was incorporated into No.5 BD Coy RE, which was commanded by Major C. Meade and was responsible for the area north of the River Thames, whilst No.2 BD Coy RE with Headquarters in Balham was responsible for the area south of the river. It shows the high ratio of UXBs which were dropped when it is realised that No. 5 BD Coy RE had dealt with 470 UXBs during the period 10th to 30th September 1940 and still had 652 incidents to be cleared on 1st October 1940. The men in the section were working very long hours, generally from 08.00hrs in the morning until 20.00 hours each evening, seven days a week. We had no time for leisure or the niceties of life.Unfortunately we had many casualties due to bombs having been fitted with delayed action fuses, and also our ignorance on the workings of many of the other types of fuses the Germans were using.

Whilst working from Wanstead we recovered many UXBs in the Romford, Dagenham, West Ham, Ilford, Stepney and Barking areas. On one occasion we were excavating for a bomb in the rear garden of a semi-detached house in Seven Kings Road Ilford, and we had excavated down to 15 feet when we discovered the tail fins, from which we were able to identify the bomb as a 250 kg. Further digging to uncover the bomb was undertaken so that the fuse or fuses could be identified, but luck was not on our side, the bomb had come to rest at an angle and the fuse pocket or pockets were concealed on the underside of the bomb. Attempts to move it by means of ropes and block and tackle secured to our 3 ton lorry parked in the adjacent road proved fruitless, we could not dislodge it. As it was getting late in the evening it was decided to call it a day, and go back the following morning and excavate further around the bomb.

We returned early the following morning, and to our horror found that the bomb had exploded, demolishing four houses and damaging many more. The local residents informed us that the bomb had exploded 15 minutes after we had left the site. This luck, if one can call it luck, or perhaps fate, did repeat itself on other occasions during my six years in bomb disposal. One assumed that the bomb had been fitted with a (17) clockwork fuse, which was designed to detonate the bomb from anytime between zero to plus 84 hours. Through disturbing the bomb, we had obviously restarted the clock. It was a common fault with this type of fuse as with other clockwork mechanisms to stop on running down, unfortunately the slightest movement of the bomb would restart the clock which normally would have little time left to run before activating the bomb.

During our first few months in London the only piece of equipment available to us in dealing with the German bomb fuse was known as the "Crabtree" two pin discharger, this was placed over the boss of the fuse and in turn depressed the two plungers, which earthed the electrical charge stored in the condensers and so rendered the fuse inert. This piece of equipment however could have distrastrous results if used on any other fuse other than the (15) Impact fuse.

On looking back after 55 years I cannot recall being concerned about one's safety when digging down to a bomb. The thought that it could explode never apparently crossed one's mind. How naive we were in our youth!

Whether we survived depended in many cases on luck. Once a fuse had been identified it was our knowledge and expertise to be able to de-fuse it on which our life depended. During the early days of 1940 the life expectancy of a Bomb Disposal Officer was approximately ten weeks.

I was working in an excavation in the town centre of Ilford one day, when completely out of the blue a German plane appeared, it came swooping down over the road with machine guns blazing as it roared past. I was taking my turn in digging in the excavation, whilst the rest of the working party had taken shelter in a nearby doorway. At that precise moment the bottom of the excavation caved in, and that is all I can remember. I was told later that the men seeing my head disappear had rushed across the road and managed to get me out of the excavation, which fortunately was shallow. I was unconscious having inhaled Carbon Monoxide gas. When I regained consciousness I was lying in a bed in Ilford Hospital with the worst headache I could ever recall. I had again been extremely lucky.

This incident had been caused by a small 50 kg bomb having penetrated the earth, but the detonation had not been strong enough to rupture the surface and form a crater, instead it formed a "sealed chamber" commonly known as a "Camouflet". Subsequently orders were issued stating that anyone working in an excavation had to have a life line tied around the waist, the free end being secured to a picket at ground level.

Between September 1940 and the 11th January 1941 air-raids were a nightly occurrence. During this period of time 14,755 High Explosive bombs and 40,860 bomb canisters containing Incendiary bombs were dropped over the London area. Each Incendiary canister contained 36 Incendiary bombs. Whilst working from Wanstead we were called out to a cemetery at Leytonstone where a stick of four unexploded bombs had been reported. For four bombs to have failed to detonate on impact pointed to either the plane having been too low when the pilot had released the bombs, or he had jettisoned the bombs without them being charged, perhaps he wanted to lighten his load to get away from a harrassing fighter plane. As mentioned earlier the German bomb fuse was electrically operated. When the bomb is secured in the bomb racks, a collett is placed over the fuse boss which permits an electrical charge to be passed into the condensers in the fuse via the plungers and resistors, prior to the

15

bomb being released. As the bomb descends this charge filters through to the firing condenser, on impact a trembler switch is activated and makes the contact, which fires the gaine, which in turn detonates the bomb. If the plane is too low when the bomb is released the trembler switch would have made the contact before the electric charge had reached the firing condenser.

On arrival at the site of the first UXB it was noted that it had penetrated the earth via the centre of a grave. Digging commenced and before long we came upon the first corpse which was in a very advanced state of decomposition. The stench was overpowering, so we resorted to pouring creosote around the walls of the excavation to neutralise the smell. The bones were lifted carefully up on our shovels and laid at ground level. The bomb when found was a 50 kg. with a No. 15 Impact fuse, which was rendered inert by the use of a "Crabtree" discharger. Having removed the bomb we replaced the corpses back into their resting place and filled back the hole. We then carried onto the next grave and repeated the operation. One of the most gruesome jobs in bomb disposal had been successfully completed. Whilst at Wanstead we had a hair raising experience when a Lance Corporal Evans who hailed from Leeds returned to our billets one evening with a 250 kg. bomb in the back of a 15 cwt truck. This bomb was fitted with a (17) delayed action fuse which could have exploded at any time. On reporting this to Lieut. Godsmark, this officer dashed to the truck, jumped into the driver's seat and drove at breakneck speed to Hackney Marshes where he rolled the bomb off the back of the truck before beating a hasty retreat. Fortunately during this time there was very little traffic on the roads of London.

Having spent four weeks in the East End of London we moved on the 3rd October to Gordon Avenue, Stanmore, to work in the areas of Wembley, Kilburn, Harrow and Chiswick. This in effect was to be a rest period, following the time we had spent under heavy pressure in the East End.

In November 1940 Lieut. Godsmark left us to join the Earl of Suffolk on experimental work and he was replaced by Lieut. Richards MC,

RE. During the six months ending in March 1941, the Earl of Suffolk visited us on many occasions to inspect and de-fuse bombs on which we were working. He had a very attractive Secretary who always accompanied him on these missions. She would stand at the edge of the excavation, and would record in shorthand the procedures he was adopting in his efforts to render the fuse safe. He would at times use a doctor's Stethoscope to check for any movement in the fuse.

Much later BD Sections were issued with electrical Stethoscopes, which enabled one to sit at a safe distance to check for any movement. The Earl and his Secretary were killed on the 12th May 1941 on Hackney Marshes whilst he was attempting to remove a fuse from a bomb using a hammer and chisel.

Whilst stationed at Stanmore we dealt with bombs in Honeypot Lane, Queensbury and at the Milk Dairy on Western Avenue. On the 11th March 1941 the section moved to Cadogan Gardens and the Duke of York's Barracks, Kings Road, Chelsea. On the night of 8/9th March the Luftwaffe renewed its raids on London. Some 125 planes took part and dropped 130 tonnes of High Explosive bombs and 24,948 Incendiary bombs on the Capital. It was during this raid that the popular Café-de-Paris restaurant in Piccadilly was hit causing many casualties. On the 19th April, London was again the target. This time 712 aircraft took part, the first phase was fairly scattered over the Capital due to heavy cloud, the second phase concentrated over the dock areas of East London from Beckton Gas Works to Tower Bridge, although areas as far afield as Acton and Harrow were hit. This attack turned out to be the heaviest of the war. 1026 tonnes of High Explosive Bombs and 153,100 Incendiary bombs were dropped. During this raid a number of Incendiary bombs fell on the Duke of York's Barracks in Chelsea and we spent most of the night putting out fires and dealing with those that had failed to ignite. From our base in Chelsea we were working in the areas of the West End, Victoria, Kensington, Chelsea and Fulham, and on one occasion we dealt with bombs in Green Park and also one which had landed in the rear gardens to

Buckingham Palace. Two UXBs at Victoria Station gave us cause for concern, one had landed on the lines just outside the station concourse and had been classified as a "A" priority bomb. We made arrangements for railway wagons filled with ballast to be shunted into place on the lines either side of "The hole of entry". Digging to re-cover this bomb started immediately and continued until we recovered a 250 kg bomb fitted with a (25) fuse. The other bomb fell in the road outside the station close to the "Windsor Dive" a noted hostelry. Both these bombs were taken to our bomb cemetery in Richmond Park where the explosive filling was steamed out.

After twelve months of intense activity in which 35 Bomb Disposal Section had dealt with over 100 UXBs we moved on the 3rd September to 60, Creffield Road, Acton, where the other sections forming No. 5 BD Coy RE, were stationed, (Sections 15, 17, 20, 21, 33, 35, 38, 54, 60, and 64.)

During the following months work was undertaken in recovering various UXBs and "Ack Ack" shells which had been placed in a low category during the height of the Blitz.

During our twelve months on active service dealing with UXBs in London it was particularly noticable that the "Cockney" in the East End was most appreciative of the work being undertaken by bomb disposal personnel. No matter how poor the neighbourhood these people who had endured the heaviest air raids during the Blitz, invariably made a collection amongst themselves, and this money was given in gratitude to the men in the BD Squad who had successfully removed an UXB from their midst. Despite the amount of damage inflicted on London it became evident that unless major key installations such as railway stations, electric power stations, gas works and other essential communications were destroyed the German Air-Force could not succeed in bringing London to a standstill. The Luftwaffe's limitation in planes meant that they were unable to totally destroy a city the size of London. They were entirely dependent on medium range twin engined bombers with a limitation on their bomb loads. The only other planes available to them in

During the raid on London on 13th December 1940 a number of bombs fell on Buckingham Palace and the surrounding areas. This picture shows the excavation in Green Park from where a 500 kg unexploded bomb was successfully defused and removed.
(Photos: R. Matkin)

1940 were the single engined dive bombers. Secondly, the majority of German bombs dropped during the early raids on London were small, the 50 kg being most dominant followed by the 250 kg bomb. Parachute mines designed to be used against shipping did more damage weight for weight due to there blast effect when dropped in the closely packed streets of the East End of London.

It was only after the publicity given to men of No.5 BD Coy RE in recovering the UXB from outside St Paul's Cathedral that the German armourers began fitting an anti-handling device known as ZUS 40, under the (17) delayed action clockwork fuse. This device was designed to detonate the bomb when attempts were made to remove the fuse. Its function was to kill bomb disposers. Mention was made earlier that the bomb on the railway line at Victoria Station had been given an "A" priority. All UXBs were allocated a category as follows:

"A 1" Immediate disposal, essential to the war effort. Demolition of the bomb cannot be accepted.

"A 2" Immediate disposal, essential to the war effort. Demolition of the bomb can be accepted.

"B 2" Disposal important to the war effort and to public morale.

"C" Disposal necessary, but not urgent.

"D" To be dealt with when convenient (UXBs) in fields and open spaces.

As it had been established that the German (17) clockwork fuse could be set to detonate a bomb up to 84 hours, after leaving the aircraft, work on category "B", "C" and "D" bombs was not undertaken until a 96 hour period had elapsed, whereas category "A" bombs were dealt with immediately.

There had been no training undertaken by any of the sections due to the heavy commitment in clearing UXBs. Many of the men had gone straight into BD Sections straight from training battalions in

September 1940, so intensive weapon and field engineering training programmes were organised. Rifle firing practice was undertaken on the ranges at Pirbright, whilst field engineering took place in Osterly Park and Richmond Park. During these training programmes I was awarded my first stripe, my reward after two year's service.

Chapter Three

In 1942 Major W Parker (Paddy as he was affectionately known) took command of No. 5 BD Coy RE, at the same time a new adjutant was also appointed (Capt W Holland). These two officers were to oversee major changes within the Company. Capt Holland instituted intensive training programmes for all NCOs in drill, weapon training, fieldworks, knots & lashings etc., at the end of which I found myself gaining rapid promotion as follows:

February 1942. Promoted to Corporal.

March 1942. Promoted to Lance- Sergeant.

April 1942. Promoted to Full Sergeant.

After my promotion to Sergeant I was sent on numerous courses, and on each occasion prior to leaving the Company, Captain Holland would say "Remember, you pass the course with "Distinction" or I will have you posted on your return." Whether it was a threat or otherwise I never found out, as fortunately I achieved this pass mark from each course. On one occasion I was attending a course on bomb disposal at the School of Military Engineering, Ripon, when a lecturer asked the question "What makes a good Bomb Disposal Officer?" One bright NCO in the class suggested that ideally he should be single, be a fast runner, and well prepared for the "after life". If this was the criteria, then I believed I qualified. In August 1942 a posting had come through for me to join the Madras Sappers and Miners in India as a Staff Sergeant. This posting was turned down by Major Parker, who in his reply to the War Office stated "This NCO is a potential Officer Cadet and is therefore not eligible for posting." In September 1942, No. 5 BD Coy RE was posted to Northern Ireland but I was kept back and given the task under Captain Holland of training a complete new intake, which became the new 5 BD Coy RE. I cannot recall what designation was given to the personnel on their arrival in Ireland.

In October Major Parker suggested that I should give some consideration to the idea of applying for a Commission. After giving his suggestion much thought and bearing in mind all my old friends and comrades had been posted to Northern Ireland, I decided to have a crack at it. I was taken in due course by Captain Holland to meet Colonel Bateman (CO No. 1 BD Group). He asked why I wanted a Commission, then proceeded to ask if I thought I was capable of building railways out in the desert etc. etc. I, however, successfully passed this initial interview, and in due course I was called to attend a three day assessment course at No. 11 War Office Selection Board (WOSB) at Golders Green. At the termination of the course I was interviewed by a Brigadier who told me that I had passed the course and that he was recommending me for a Commission in the Royal Artillery, to which I replied, "No Sir, if I cannot be commissioned into the Royal Engineers then I would prefer to return to my unit as a Sergeant". I will never know whether this was a test of my determination, but I did go to 140 OCTU, RE, based at Newark, where after six months intensive training I received my Commission in August 1943.

On receiving my Commission I was granted seven days leave, at the end of which I had to report to a CRE at Darlington. On arrival I reported to him and was informed that I was awaiting a posting to India, but in the meantime he was to utilise my services. He told me about the various Units under his command, i.e:- Airfield

Construction Coys, Field Coys, and a Bomb Disposal Coy, and asked which unit I would like to spend my time pending my posting. I informed him that prior to going to OCTU I had served most of my time in bomb disposal in London, and although I had been trained at OCTU for service in a Field Coy, I would like to await my posting with a BD Coy. He arranged for me to join No 14 BD Coy RE, which had its headquarters in Leeds. This company was responsible for the removal of all UXBs in the County of Yorkshire.

On arrival in Leeds I was surprised to find the OC was none other than Major Alec Cleghorn whom I had served under in London. It is amazing to think how certain people whom I met in the army changed the direction of my career. I have related how Major Parker set me on a new path, Major Cleghorn was to have a similar effect. He arranged for my posting to India to be cancelled and appointed me OC No 11 BD Section RE. My section Sergeant was a Sgt. Quarendon who was later awarded the George Cross for outstanding bravery whilst working in Hull. Shortly after taking command of this section we went on detachment to Hull and made our headquarters in the Drill Hall, Walton Street which was off Anlaby Road.

One of my first assignments was to take over from Lieut. Richards whilst he went on leave, and to continue the work of recovering a bomb which had fallen in the Market Square during a raid on the 24th June 1943. Due to the ground conditions apertaining in Hull the recovery of this bomb was causing major problems. The Market Square was close to the River Hull, and one could literally see the rise and fall of the tide in the excavation. The ground conditions in general in Hull consisted of 18 inches of top soil, 4-00 ft of soft clay and then for the next 44-00 ft wet silt. Boulder clay was encountered at approx 46-00 ft.

Digging for this bomb commenced in July 1943 and the first shaft to be sunk measured 8-00 ft x 8-00 ft, this was taken down to a depth of 19-00 ft when due to the pressure on the timber shuttering it had to be abandoned. A second shaft was started on 6th September 1943, but again was abandoned at 19-6 ft. A third shaft was started

on 22nd October 1943 measuring 10-00 ft x10-00 ft. This was the
̶ ̶ ̶avation I was responsible for. It reached 23-00 ft and parts of
alloy tail fin was found at this depth. The pressure of the wet silt
he timber shuttering again forced the abandonment of this shaft.
ourth shaft measuring 17-6 ft x 15-00 ft this time using Larssen
:l sheet piling was started on 24th February 1944 but again had
e abandoned at 28-00 ft. A further shaft was started on 1st June
4, pumps were manned 24 hours a day to keep the water table at
icceptable level to allow the excavation to proceed. A small rail
:k was laid so that excavated material could be taken some
ance from the excavation and so reduce the surcharge on the
ft walls.

it. Richards persisted with this operation and I heard later that
iad sunk a sixth shaft down to 33-00 ft before he was rewarded
:covering a 1,000 kg (Herman) bomb on 2nd February 1946.
ing taken three years to recover this must rank as the longest
rt in the history of bomb disposal.

the 17/18th August 1943 there had been a heavy air-raid on
ll and the surrounding areas, when a great number of "Butterfly
mbs" had been dropped. For many weeks after this raid we were
l searching in hedgerows, cornfields and ditches in the Hedon
l Hornsea areas for these lethal fragmentation bombs. We resorted
placing straw in the ditches and firing it to clear the thick
entanglement of undergrowth. Once cleared we placed a small
charge on the casing of the bomb and detonated it. These small
anti-personnel bombs weighed approx four and a half pounds. 24
of these bombs were packed into a light steel canister which
resembled a bomb and was fitted with a (89) fuse. This was an air-
burst fuse with a possible two minute delay. It detonated a small
charge which burst open the container some two minutes after
leaving the aircraft. Once the container was opened the "Butterfly
Bombs" proceeded by the use of their drogues to earth. These bombs
consisted of two parts, the main fragmentation body, which
contained the explosive charge and a light steel metal outer casing
which was in four segments and enveloped the main body of the
bomb; to which it was attached by a short wire cable to the arming

ERRATUM. Page 24 Sergeant G Quarendon ̶ ̶ ̶ awarded the George Medal

spindle of the fuse. The two half cylinders of the casing formed a pair of wings to slow down the ascent. The two end sections formed a propellor, the rotation of which caused the wire cable which was screwed into the fuse to rotate. When the spindle had been unscrewed approx. four turns the fuse was armed. Three types of fuse could be fitted to these bombs, namely (41) for detonation on impact, (67) a delayed action clockwork mechanism which was armed in flight and (70) which was an anti-handling fuse.

No. 11 BD Section undertook the recovery of a bomb which had landed in an open area behind Saltcoates Road, in the dock area of Hull. A standard 8-00 ft x 8-00ft shaft was timbered down to a depth of 20-00ft and the same wet conditions which were encountered in the Market Square were present. Pumps again had to be used 24 hours a day to keep the water at a level in which the men could work.

On my arrival at the site the Corporal in charge of the working party reported that they had uncovered the bomb, but because the head of the fuse had been damaged he was unable to identify it. I attached the electrical stethoscope to the bomb casing and ascertained that there was no ticking, but what type of fuse had been fitted? It could be a "Y" fuse which incorporated two globules of mercury, which if the bomb was disturbed after landing would roll together to make the contact and so detonate the bomb. This fuse was specifically designed to kill bomb disposal personnel. The only certain fact I had was the bomb was a 250kg, with a single fuse fitted. I decided therefore to take an "X Ray" photograph of the fuse pocket and so the necessary equipment was called up. This equipment consisted of a frame which clamped around the bomb. A photographic plate was placed on one side and a seedling of Radium on the opposite side. Several hours of darkness was necessary to obtain an "X Ray" photograph through the metal casing of the bomb and its filling and ultimately the fuse pocket.

I remember clearly setting up the equipment on a Saturday evening with every intention of getting a print on the Sunday morning. As is wont to happen with mechanical equipment the pump broke down

during the night and the excavation filled with water. The hoped
for print was black and useless.

It was time for a decision to be made: does one wait another 24
hours and repeat the operation, or go against the rule book? I decided
to attempt the removal of the fuse. With my Sergeant at the safety
point and listening for any ticking from the fuse via the electric
stethoscope which had been attached to the bomb casing I collected
the Merrylees fuse extractor and approached the shaft. I descended
down to the bomb. It was so quiet and peaceful. The only sound
was the water dripping off the timber shuttering and the beat of my
heart. I clearly remember thinking that should the bomb explode, I
would know nothing about it, death would be instantaneous. Slowly,
I removed the fuse locking ring and noted there was no tendency
for the fuse to "pop up". I then positioned the Merrylees fuse
extractor into the threads which had been previously used to hold
the locking ring in position. The threaded rod with a collet on one
end was attached to the fuse head, at the other end of the threaded
rod a drum on which a length of cord was wound. I then screwed
some eyelets into the timber shuttering at suitable points to ensure
that the cord from the extractor would run smoothly and freely. I
carefully unwound a length of the cord from the drum and threaded
it through the eyelets and up to the safety point. Once at the safety
point I pulled slowly on the cord, waiting for the inevitable
explosion. Still peaceful. After I had wound in a considerable length
of cord, I reckoned the fuse must have been extracted from the fuse
pocket. I waited a short period of time before approaching the
excavation. I climbed down, then wound the cord back onto the
drum, unscrewed the fuse extractor cylinder and there safely inside
was the fuse. I unscrewed the Gaine from the base of the fuse and
climbed back up. The men could now get on with the job of
removing the bomb, removing the shuttering and back filling the
hole. Another UXB dealt with successfully, and so onto the next
one.

Now after 50 years one thinks back and wonders why with all my
experience didn't I wait a further 24 hours and attempt to obtain an

"X Ray" of the fuse. Let us put it down to youthful impatience, and again I had got away with it.

In October the section returned to Headquarters in Leeds and later that month I attended an Assault Training Course at Llanberis, North Wales. This was a very intensive course in Infantry Tactics. One of the exercises we had to undertake was to swim across Lake Padern in "Battle Order". With boots and rifle slung around the neck, we scrambled out on the far bank and dripping wet continued into Snowdonia undertaking battle exercises using live ammunition. We didn't kill any of the men on the course, but we did kill a few sheep concealed in the heather. The instructors often said during the course, you may be dead before you are 45 years old with rheumatism etc, but we can guarantee your fitness when you leave here! I returned to Leeds 100 percent fit.

With the knowledge and experience acquired on this course I became Training Officer to the Company and passed on my knowledge to all sections in 14 BD Coy RE between November 1943 and March 1944 at the camp based at Raby Castle, Staindrop, Co. Durham.

In April 1944 I was selected to attend a series of specialised courses. Ten BD Officers had been brought together. We did not know at the time the purpose of this training, but it soon became apparent that it was leading up to something very special.

We began by attending a four week "Field Engineering" course at the School of Military Engineering, Ripon. Whilst at Ripon I was promoted to Full Lieutenant. At the end of this course I returned to my Company in Leeds and took Command of No. 11 BD Section. At the end of May we all assembled in London and received instruction on the "Recognition and Disposal of British and American Bombs". On my return to Leeds I took Command of No. 171 BD Section effective from 3rd June 1944. Why I was transferred from No 11 Section, I cannot recall the reason. On the 11th June our training was to be undertaken by the Royal Navy. On this date the "Special Ten" assembled at the Royal Naval Gunnery School, Chatham. On the morning following our arrival we were given a medical examination, after which we were taken out by boat onto

German SD 2 anti-personnel bomb.
(the Butterfly bomb)

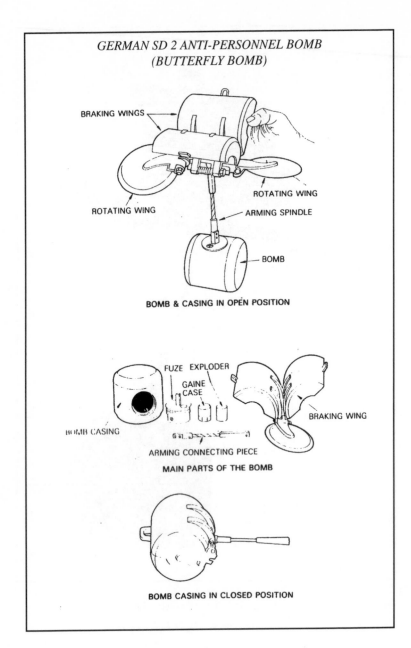

GERMAN SD 2 ANTI-PERSONNEL BOMB
(BUTTERFLY BOMB)

BRAKING WINGS

ROTATING WING

ROTATING WING

ARMING SPINDLE

BOMB

BOMB & CASING IN OPEN POSITION

FUZE EXPLODER

GAINE
CASE

BOMB CASING

BRAKING WING

ARMING CONNECTING PIECE

MAIN PARTS OF THE BOMB

BOMB CASING IN CLOSED POSITION

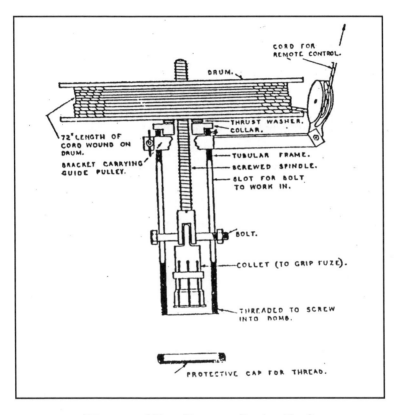

Diagram of Fuze Extractor Design No. 2.

the River Medway. We were introduced to the Siebe Gorman heavy diving suit, this consisted of a canvas suit and copper helmet. We took it in turns assisted by naval ratings to don the suit, after which they secured heavy lead weights on our back and chest. Finally they placed heavy lead boots on our feet. We were then led to a ladder which hung over the side of the boat. Once on the ladder the copper helmet was secured and finally the face glass was screwed into position.

We were given the "Thumbs Down" signal to descend into the murky depths of the River Medway. One controlled their descent and ascent by means of an "air valve" fitted on the side of the helmet. This was a tricky operation until one got accustomed to it, on occasions we floated up to the surface like a fully inflated balloon and generally face down. After making many dives into a 32-00 ft depth of water we were ready to take our examination. Various tasks had to be performed on the river bed, such as unravelling chains, bolting up steel box sections etc,etc. We all passed the course as competent divers. On the 16th July 1944 we were again the guests of the Royal Navy, as we joined HMS Volcano which was a shore establishment based at Holmbrook Hall, Drigg, Cumbria. Here we received instruction on the workings of the German antiship mines and how to render them safe. The course incorporated training in the use of the self contained diving suit, and diving took place in the River Chet whose waters were crystal clear, very different from those encountered in the River Medway.

On the 2nd August 1944 I was at Company Headquarters in Leeds, when a telephone call came through in the evening informing me that there had been an accident in a minefield at Redcar where a brother officer and his section were engaged in its clearance. I called for my driver/batman to get some kit together and also to bring my PU Truck over to the Officers Mess. We set out for Redcar arriving late in the evening. There was little I could do at such a late hour. My first priority was to ensure that the perimeter fence around the minefield had been put back in position and secured. The officer together with his sergeant and two sappers had been killed, the rest of his men were in deep shock. I was told that their bodies were still in the minefield. I instructed the men to go to bed and try and get some sleep and I would see them in the morning. The following morning I obtained some tin cans and buried them on a strip of spare ground adjacent to the Drill Hall in which they were billeted. I then got the men together and gave them a period of instruction on the use of the mine detector. This exercise was to restore their confidence in the equipment before taking them back into the minefield. I wanted no more casualties. A stretcher party was organised to follow me into the minefield. I swept a clear passage which was marked by two sappers following behind me and marking the path with white tapes. We collected their remains, which were then taken to the local mortuary. That evening I attended an inquest and obtained death certificates for those killed. I also made arrangements for the coffins to be weighted before they were released to their next of kin. Most of the minefield had erupted thus creating a massive job to ascertain the number of mines left and still to be cleared. Some other officer was going to have that head-ache.

On the 8th August 1941, I made my third visit to a Royal Naval establishment. On this occasion I was attending a course at HMS Vernon, Portsmouth, on how to neutralize British and German anti-ship mines. At the end of this course a number of my fellow Officers went over to France and later into Germany dealing with UXBs and also minefield clearance.

On the 21st August 1944, Lieut. Eric Wakeling and I took part in a sound ranging experiment under the directions of Northern Command. We each had to collect 2 tonnes of gun-cotton from a depot in North Yorkshire. I had to proceed to Spurn Point at the mouth of the River Humber, whilst he to a rendezvous point on the moors above Whitby. The distance between the two points was 70 miles, and we had to detonate our charges at exactly midnight. The experiment was to measure the sound waves so created. Lieut. Wakeling has often wondered what size crater he created, as he left the site before day-break. He does however recall that it rained the whole time they were at Whitby and that they cooked their supper inside the 3 ton truck beside the explosive.

On the 9th September 1944 I returned to Leeds from the Training Camp at Staindrop, and on the 18th September I was posted to Command No.24 Bomb Disposal Platoon RE.

Bomb Disposal sections were redesignated during August 1944 as Bomb Disposal platoons.

Chapter Four

THE INVASION OF THE CHANNEL ISLANDS

The Channel Islands, which geographically have a closer affinity to France than to the United Kingdom, have the unique claim of being the only British Territory to have been occupied by the German forces during the 1939 - 1945 war.

After the German advance across France in May 1940, their closeness to the mainland of France precluded any possibility by the British Government of defending them against a German invasion. With Alderney only 7 miles and Jersey 14 miles off the French coast, all the islands were within shelling distance from gun batteries sited on the French coast. This led to the British Government's decision to de-militarise them. On the 20th June 1940 all the regular British troops stationed on the islands were withdrawn. Because of the prevarication of the British Government, the German Government was not informed that the military evacuation had been completed.

On this same date the German High Command issued the following order. "Occupation of the British Channel Islands is both urgent and important, carry out local reconnaissance and execution thereof." The invasion by sea of the islands had been drawn up under the code name "Green Arrow". Naval assault groups together with units of 216 Infantry Division were allotted to this task force. For ten days the Germans had been attempting to establish whether the islands would be defended. Reconnaissance flights over the islands by the Luftwaffe at 10,000 feet could not positively establish the situation, there were no signs of any white flags being flown. At 6.45 pm on the 28th June 1940, they decided to carry out an armed reconnaissance over Jersey and Guernsey, the activities of the evacuation of some 17,000 islanders, and also the loading of tomatoes and potatoes were misconstrued by the German pilots as troop movements. Some 180 bombs were dropped on the Harbour installations in St. Helier and St. Peter Port. 44 civilians were killed in these two raids, 34 in St. Peter Port and 10 in St. Helier.

The original plan drawn up by the German Command for the capture of the Channel Islands was for the Kriegsmarine to be in command of the operation, but whilst the invasion troops were being assembled at Cherbourg, the pilot of a Dornier DO 17, who had been flying a reconnaissance mission over Guernsey on Sunday 30th June 1940, noted that there was no visible activity around the aerodrome, so decided to land, whilst the other three planes in his flight circled overhead. He found the aerodrome completely deserted. On his return to Cherbourg, Admiral Lindau, who was responsible for the invasion of the islands was acquainted with the fact that the island was undefended, he therefore issued orders for the immediate occupation of Guernsey. At about 7.30 pm the first transport plane landed on Guernsey with a platoon of airforce troops. At about 2.45pm on Monday 1st July 1940 a further transport plane landed and those aboard included Major Albrecht Lanz, military Commandant designate. He was taken into St. Peter Port where he met the Bailiff and other state officials, who were informed by him that he would be in Command of the island with immediate effect. The same day a naval detachment and a company of infantry taken from 216 Infantry Division who had been waiting in Cherbourg to launch the invasion by sea were moved to a nearby airfield and flown to the island. Thus, for the first time in many centuries, an invading force had set foot on British soil. Hitler considered the capture of the islands as a jewel in his crown.

Although the occupation of the island had been undertaken, life on Guernsey carried on much as normal apart from the presence of German troops. The islanders were allowed to attend church services and prayers were offered up for the Royal Family, but in return the Bailiff agreed to register as law the orders of the German Command. This procedure gave the Bailiff an illusion of power. He believed that by serving the Germans he was running their occupation for them. For some time the illusion was sustained, the Germans who were so confident of victory were scrupulously correct in their dealings with the islanders and the population responded.

Very quickly the Germans began to consolidate their position in the island as reinforcements from 216 Infantry Division and 396 Infantry Division were sent to the islands. Many of these troops believed they were on the Isle of Wight. On the 2nd July 1940, an order was issued by the German Commandant, Major A. Lanz, which set out the procedures to be adopted by the Islands Administration and this set the seal for the control of the island for the next five years.

Immediately following the occupation, Winston Churchill ordered that reconnaissance raids be undertaken to assess the strength of the German garrison on the island. On the 6th July 1940 just six days after the Germans had arrived on the island the first British troops were put ashore. Similar small raiding parties were put ashore during the August and September. These reconnaissance parties were landed by submarine on the small beaches on the South Coast, and were able to proceed ashore by means of the paths and lanes which led from these beaches. To have attempted these raids some twelve months later when 319 Infantry Division had laid down the minefields, which formed a continuous defence for the full length of the South Coast and also had secured 1,000 Roll Bombs on the cliff faces would have been suicidal. After 1940 no further raids were carried out against Guernsey.

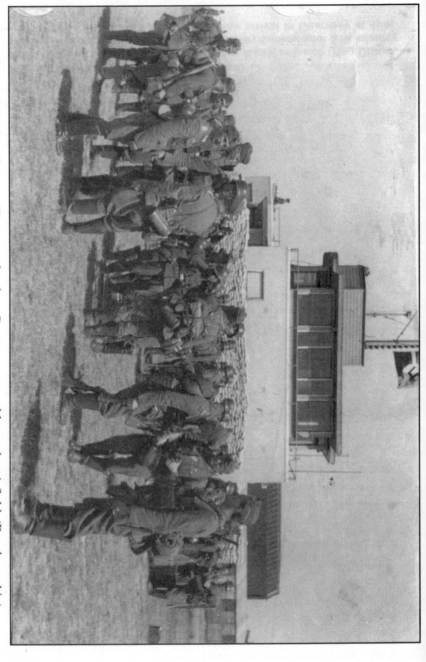

Some of the first German Troops to land on Guernsey assemble on the airfield. (Bundesarchiv)

Some of the first German Troops which were transported to the Island on the 1st July 1940, unloading from a Junker's transport aircraft. (Bundesarchiv)

Major Dr. A. Lanz, A doctor of Law and Philosophy, the first military commander of Guernsey 1st July to 18th September 1940. He was killed on the Russian front in the war.

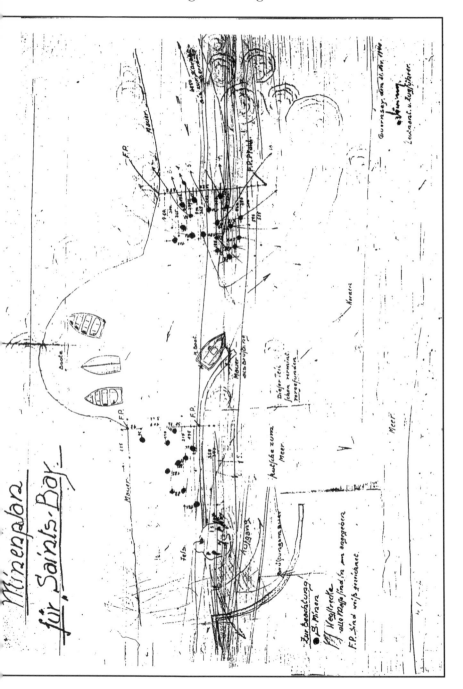

These raids gave great displeasure to the Bailiff and other leading dignatories on the island. The Bailiff Victor Carey condemned these raids as futile and in Official Documents refers to the British as "The Enemy". The President of the Controlling Committee, A.J. Sherwill, went as far as to draft a letter on the 18th July 1940 to the Home Office in which he stated that military activities of this kind were most unwelcome, and that the islanders should be left in peace and allowed to get on with their lives. However the German Command refused to co-operate with him, so the letter was never received in London. The German confidence of victory was such that even after the raids on the South coast of the island immediately following their occupation they made no attempt to put down any major fortifications. The German High Command's first priority was the invasion of England which was planned for September 1940 under the code name "Sealion", but this date was continually being revised due to the activity of the RAF against the barges being assembled along the French coast. It was not until the 20th November 1940 that men from 216 Infantry Division laid the first mines which consisted of 21 "S" Mines (Schrapnellmine). These were laid in the approach lane to Fermain Bay. During the next six weeks a further 124 mines were laid in small clusters in the exit lanes leading from Saints Bay, Moulin Huet and La Corbiere, then the whole operation came to a standstill. It was in these areas that the raiding parties had landed during the preceeding months. The plan for Saints Bay shows how the mines were laid to protect the exit from the beach.

In general resistance on the part of Guernsey men was seldom, if ever, attempted, their excuse being that there was nowhere to hide or escape to, and such actions would only bring serious reprisals against the population generally. From day one the islanders welcomed the German occupying forces, fraternisation was rife within all sections of the community. Island women solaced themselves with German lovers. The blonde German was much preferred to the male islander who was considered dour and in consequence and inevitably the number of illegitimate births soared. The numbers of births registered as illegitimate were recorded only for single women. Married women who bore children fathered by German troops were recorded under their husband's name as legitimate even though he could have been serving in the British Forces, and therefore the records do not give an accurate picture of the total number of illegitimate births which occured during the occupation.

I had first hand experience of this problem when one of my men asked my permission to marry an islander whom he claimed was pregnant by him, on checking this out I found that this woman had already two children who had been fathered by German troops. I arranged for this Sapper to be on the next boat to England for a posting to another area as far away as possible from the Channel Islands. Whether he ever appreciated my actions I will never know. The Island Government formed a close relationship with the Germans and carried out all their orders. On the 15th September 1942 the Germans published an order stating that all men not born

Fraternisation was widespread throughout the island.

on the Channel Islands between the ages of 16 to 70 years of age and their families would be evacuated to Germany. The German Administration requested the Island Government to prepare lists of these British born subjects who were then rounded up by the island police force and shipped off to concentration camps at Wurzach and Biberach. Life on the island went along generally very peacefully, food was sufficient, as adequate supplies were being shipped in from France via Granville and St. Malo. Most of the islanders did not consider the occupation a difficult time. Life was quiet and mostly boring. Relationships with the Germans was no cause for comment because most islanders either were friendly with them or had serious relationships with them. This fraternisation did not stop in the bedroom. The German authorities were greatly helped by informers and anonymous letter writers. It is reported that one German Officer received 200 letters a month from islanders informing on fellow islanders. During July 1941 the Germans discovered that "V" for victory signs had been painted on signposts and gate posts around the island. The Germans made it clear that they took an extremely serious view of this and were not prepared to tolerate such acts of provocation. The German Commandant wrote directly to the Bailiff requesting that he notify the population forthwith that any further acts of the letter "V" appearing would be treated as an act of sabotage and would be severely punished. The Bailiff took the further step of offering a reward of £25 to any person who gave the police information leading to a conviction. This reward was never claimed. The thought of selling out their fellow islanders to the enemy was most repulsive. This incident caused the Bailiff's standing throughout the island to yet again fall to a very low level. This incident again showed clearly the collaboration which existed between State Officials and the German Occupation Forces.

Over 50 percent of the population worked for the Germans either in building the many fortifications or in other services such as transport drivers, etc. The rates of pay which they received were in many cases far higher than they had received prior to the occupation. For more than two years their lives changed very little; food was plentiful and the German troops returning from leave would bring back many luxuries in the way of perfume etc, to bestow on their "lady friends". Collaboration became the norm. The Germans organised dances and various sports such as football matches; when teams made up of islanders played against teams from the German units. Entertainments particularly of an amateur nature were also arranged with the islanders participating.

The restrictions imposed on the islanders by the Germans meant they had to abide by the strict curfew laws after darkness and having been deprived of their radio sets found life very dull and boring.

The administration of the island was in the hands of a Controlling Committee with Major A.J. Sherwill as President. This committee met weekly and established a close working relationship with the German administration. The line between practicality and collaboration was very close. In June 1941 when Germany invaded Russia, Hitler was seized with the fear that the British would take action behind his back in the West. He believed that the Channel Islands might be used to mount an operation against France, so he issued orders to General Marshall Gerd Von Rundstedt (Supreme Commander, West) that the defences of the islands had to be strengthened. In July he demanded that the army unit on the islands be brought up to divisional strength. On the Cotentin peninsular General Erich Marcks, who commanded LXXXIV Corps, had five divisions under his Command for the defence of the Cherbourg peninsular, one of which was 319 Infanterie Division. This division of some 36,000 men was moved to the Islands in July 1941 to replace 216 Infantry Division which was transferred to the Russian front. Work was to be undertaken in providing at least 200 strongpoints in Jersey and Guernsey. Heavy coastal batteries had to be installed, minefields laid, and all the beaches had to be secured against a sea landing by the installation of under water obstacles, mined tetrahedra etc. Roll bombs were to be suspended along the cliff tops ready for release should a landing be made at the base of the cliffs. Flame throwers were to be positioned at road junctions and other strategic points. Obstructions in the form of poles fitted with explosive charges were to be extensively used over the islands interior to prevent parachute and glider landings.

The islands were to be converted into a vast building site. 16,000 workers, mainly Russian and Polish prisoners of war, were to be shipped to the islands to work under the direction of the "TODT" organisation. This labour force was to dig tunnels into the rock, construct gun emplacements, bunkers etc. and literally turn the islands into an impregnable fortress. On Guernsey the "Mirus" battery consisting of four 48 ton 12 inch guns were sited at St Saviour's, and in addition there were 14 Coastal batteries and 33 anti-aircraft batteries sited around the island. In short, the islands became the most heavily defended in the whole of Europe. The engineer battalion of 319 Infantry Division was commanded by Hauptman Kias. This unit began to lay its first minefield consisting of 189 "S" mines at Fort Le Marchant on the 27th October 1941. Minefield laying continued on the Western promontories and 3393 "S" mines and 8 "Tellermines" were laid at Fort Saumarez, Fort Richmond, Fort Hommet, Port Soif, Pulias, Infer and Rousse before the year was out. The work continued unabated throughout 1942, when a further 9,222 "S" mines and 964 "Tellermines" were laid along the cliff tops of the South Coast. The following year saw the first introduction of "Improvised" mines which were of wooden construction similar in detail to the "Schu" Mine (an abbreviation of "Schutzenmine") but were designed by 319 Infantry Division and designated as "Behelfsminen/B2" and "Behelfsminen/ B4" Some 10,519 of these mines together with 3904 "S" mines and 512 Tellermines were laid during 1943. These two particular antipersonnel mines were used extensively to form protective minefields around the gun batteries of "Mirus", Rinozerous, Barbara, Steinbruch and Elefant and also around the airfield where some 4,000 were placed around the perimeter. In 1944 a further 43,842 mines were laid, the bulk of which were "S" and "Schu" mines. This same year existing minefields were strengthened, and gaps were filled in along the coast. A further 1082 "S" mines were laid at L'Eree. (Minefield No. 113) and an additional 1452 "S" mines were introduced into Minefield No. 112 adjacent to St. Sampson's Harbour. The last minefield (No. 54) consisting of 31 "S" mines was laid at Jerbourg on 23rd March 1945 some six weeks before Liberation Day. In all there were 115 minefields put down on Guernsey containing 72,566 mines. In 1944 the Germans lifted 6,110 mines from 21 minefields so that other fortifications could be built on the sites previously occupied by them. This left a balance of 66,456, spread over 94 minefields to be dealt with by the Liberation forces. The piers and jetties in St Peter Port and St. Sampson, were prepared for demolition using 27 cm, captured French shells placed around the concrete columns.

All the beaches on the North, West and East coasts were obstructed with anti-tank girders set in the sand and wired to shells and mines to protect against the landing of tanks and landing craft. Low lying areas adjacent to the beaches were protected by large concrete anti-tank walls. Examples of these can still be seen in L'Ancresse and Vazon Bays. It is no over statement to say that the Channel Islands were the most heavily fortified areas in Europe. When the invasion of France took place in June 1944 the islands were by-passed by the Allied forces, this caused problems in regards to feeding the civilian population and the German forces. Their previously adequate food and material supplies from France were severed, hence food was becoming in very short supply. In an attempt to ease the problem the Germans evacuated all the foreign workers in August before the port of Cherbourg fell into Allied hands. Food was becoming a major problem during the last six months of 1944, there was a flourishing black market in supplies being smuggled in from France, the farmers and those living in the country areas fared much better than those living in the towns. With the island having been turned into a fortress, the islanders had another problem to face in that large tracts of the island were out of bounds. They were restricted by the curfew which came in at 8.00pm at which time the electricity was shut off, in short life was becoming very monotonous and boring.

The food situation grew progressively worse towards the end of 1944 and with the winter upon them they were rescued by the Red Cross after an urgent request sent by the German and Swedish authorities. The steamer "Vega" sailed from Lisbon with 750 tonnes of food and she arrived in St. Peter Port on the 28th December 1944. The food parcels were distributed amongst the islanders. The German troops did not receive any parcels although they were suffering from hunger. They collected nettles to make soup, and every cat and dog on the island had been eaten by them. They told me that once these had been skinned you could not tell the difference between them and a rabbit.

From September 1944 the islanders rations had been drastically cut to 500 grams of bread, 125 grams of fat, 20 grams of meat and 500 grams of potatoes per week. The German forces in comparison received 2100 grams of bread, 500 grams of meat, 245 grams of fat and 2800 grams of potatoes.

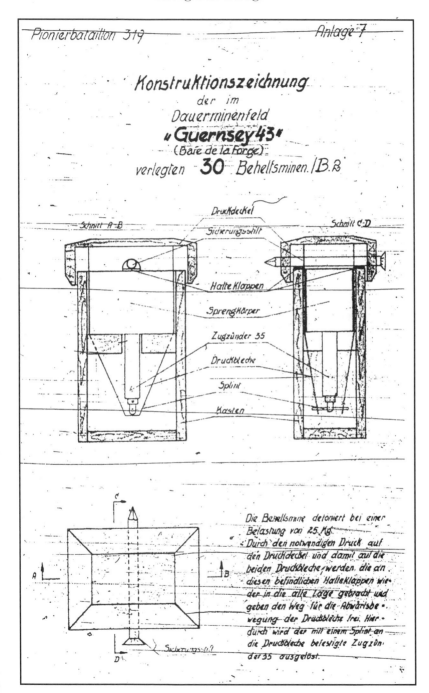

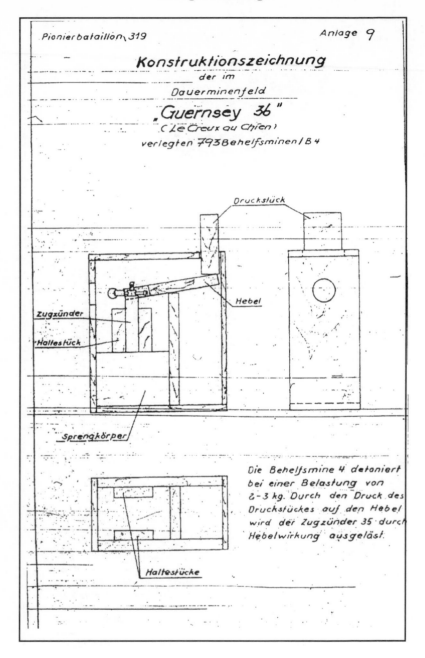

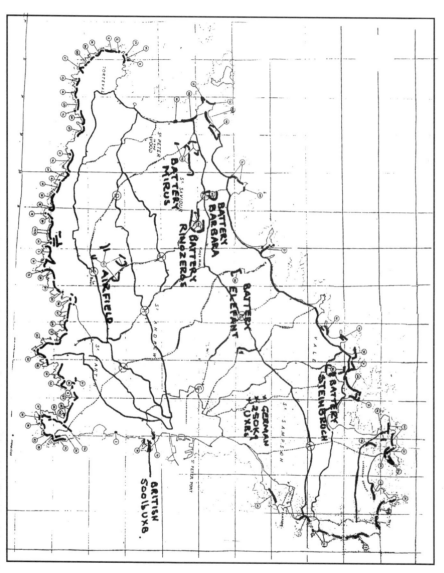

Minefield Chart, Guernsey.

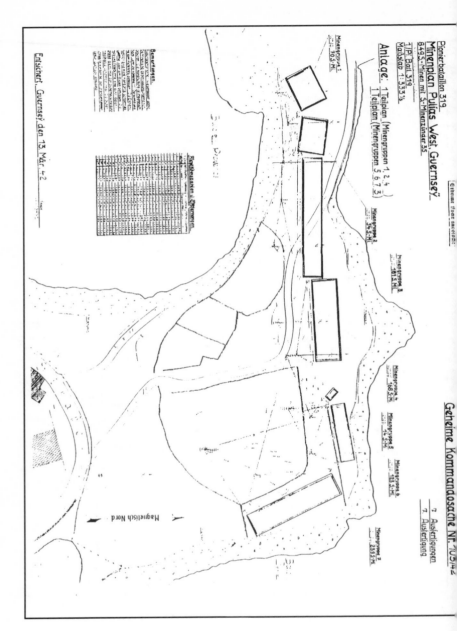

Minefield Plan No. 30 Pulias (West) Guernsey.

German Observation Tower, Pleinmont Point, Guernsey. A number of these towers were built during 1942 around the island.

Under Water Obstacles in Vazon Bay with "Tellermine." attached.

Anti-tank obstacles, L'Ancresse Bay.

Tetrahedra on beaches with Tellermine attached.

L'Ancresse Common, Anti-Landing Poles.

Fermain Bay, Underwater Obstacles.

"Hedgehogs" exposed at half tide.

New Pier St. Peter Port. No. 198 300lbs French Shells fixed to R.C. Piers as Demolition Charges.

Chapter Five

I travelled down to Plymouth and was met at the station by my new batman, (Driver Scrivener) who drove me to Fort Tregantle, Cornwall, where No. 24 Bomb Disposal Platoon RE were stationed. The Fort had been built during the Napoleonic Wars, and was complete with moat and drawbridge and was situated overlooking Cawsands Bay at the mouth of the River Tamar.

No. 24 Bomb Disposal Platoon RE had been part of No. 2 B.D. Coy RE, with its Headquarters in Balham, South London. It had been mobilised to form part of Force 135, a Task Force whose ultimate goal was to be the Liberation of the Channel Islands at some unknown date in the future. The final destination of the force had not been divulged to the rank and file.

Force 135 consisted of 6,000 men under the command of Brigadier Alfred Snow and was being assembled in the Plymouth and South Devon Area. The operation had been given the code name "NESTEGG" and the islands had been designated as "BOOTY" for Jersey and "AGENT" for Guernsey.

When the time came for the Liberation to take place the platoon would be split into two sections. One would proceed to Jersey whilst the other went to Guernsey, so the strength of the platoon had been increased to:

> One Officer
> One Sergeant
> Two Lance Sergeants
> Four Corporals
> 6 Lance Corporals
> 24 Sappers
> 5 Drivers One
> ACC Cook.

On arrival at Fort Tregantle I reported to Lieut. Colonel Wilkinson who was OC 158 CRE Works RE and also responsible for all the Royal Engineer units in Force 135. Planning for operation "NESTEGG" had commenced at the end of 1943. The Jersey contingent was to be under the command of Lieut. Colonel Robinson whilst Lieut. Colonel Stoneman commanded the Guernsey force.

As the men in this platoon were all new to me I found it necessary to assess their level of training and general competence. They had spent a comparatively easy time over the preceeding twelve months in London and this showed in the slackness of their turnout and general efficiency.

I instituted a training programme, which included route marches. I found that a ten mile march was too much for many of them, they suffered from sore and blistered feet. Gradually over the forthcoming weeks the distances covered were increased so that by the end of December 1944 they were stronger and fitter and could cover a distance of twenty miles in a day without undue effects. In addition to the training I had instituted, the platoon undertook exercises with the Infantry units in Force 135.

By the end of January 1945 the men were in peak condition both physically and also in their knowledge of mines and explosives. They were now getting bored, and bored soldiers generally find trouble to get into, so I sought permission for them to put their knowledge into practice. We were allocated a stretch of beach adjacent to the railway line running into Penzance on which a series of minefields had been laid in 1940. Here for the first time these men came face to face with the dangers of minefield clearance. The difficulties of minefield clearance around the English coastline were enormous, some mines had been washed away by the sea, others were buried under many feet of sand which had built up over five years of war, in other cases corrosion had set in on the firing springs making them extremely dangerous.

An added difficulty was that many of these minefields had been hurriedly laid in 1939/1940 by Infantry units and no proper records had been made showing the layout and spacing of mines. The majority of all mines laid were the British "B" Type "C" anti-tank mine.

I had taken over this stretch of coast-line from a Lieut. Matthews, who had been one of the "Special Ten" referred to previously. Prior to our arrival in Penzance there had been an accident in this minefield and Lieut. Matthews had been injured by shrapnel and flying sand. He had been admitted to Penzance Hospital and it was feared that he would lose his sight. Much later I learnt that he did lose his sight, but due to the excellent care and attention he received from St. Dunstan's Blind Hospital and the training he received later qualified him to practice in Law.

During our stay in Penzance I was billeted with a very charming lady who treated me as her own son. Alas her cooking left much to be desired, practically every night she served up spaghetti for dinner. Our work in Penzance was completed in February 1945, after which we returned to Fort Tregantle.

The Allied Forces had liberated France and were pushing up into Holland and Belgium the next objective would be Germany. During March and April Force 135 were rehearsing beach landings using the town of Paignton for St. Helier, and Brixham for St. Peter Port. The plan envisaged landings in St. Aubins Bay, Jersey and on the beach in L'Ancresse bay in Guernsey. A major exercise was held on 11th to 13th April which involved the loading of LSTs in Plymouth with men and vehicles and sailing round to Paignton and Brixham where they were discharged onto the beaches. With the exercise completed I took my platoon to Weymouth to undertake further minefield clearance. These minefields were situated on the cliff tops and were over grown with thick undergrowth. We had to resort to the use of flame throwers to clear it. The number of Adders, Grass snakes and Rabbits which scurried out in front of the flames had to be seen to be believed. We undertook this second minefield clearance without incurring any casualties. Our training was paying off.

With the end of the war in Europe imminent, operation "NESTEGG" was alerted on 3rd May 1945. We returned to Fort Tregantle and commenced the task of loading all our vehicles and equipment ready for sailing.

The men were issued with their shoulder flashes which depicted three rampant lions on a red shield, the coat of arms of the Channel Islands. Our destination was no longer a secret.

On the 5th May 1945 a radio message was broadcast to the Channel Islands, stating that the GOC Southern Command was authorised to receive the unconditional surrender of the German Occupying Forces. On the 6th May the German radio station at St. Peter Port acknowledged the message and replied, "The Commander in Chief, Channel Islands receives orders only from his own Government." On the 7th May a second message was sent to Vice Admiral Huffmier, who replied that his representative would rendezvous at the Les Hanois lighthouse at 12.00 hours on the 8th May.

Brigadier Snow, Commander of Force 135, sailed in HMS "Bulldog" with escort HMS "Beagle" from Plymouth to the rendezvous area. Admiral Huffmier sent a young Kapitan Lieutnant Zimmerman as his representative, who had authority only to discuss Armistice terms.

Brigadier Snow gave him a copy of the surrender document which the German High Command had signed on 7th May and advised him that there was no question of an Armistice, and that he was only prepared to accept Unconditional Surrender.

At 07.14 hours on the 9th May 1945, the instrument of surrender of the German Occupying Forces was signed on the Quarter Deck of HMS "Bulldog", by Major General Heine who was Commander of German Forces in Guernsey. The small advance party which had sailed in HMS "Bulldog" under the command of Lieut. Colonel Stoneman went ashore on the morning of 9th May to hoist the Union Jack.

In the afternoon Winston Churchill broadcast to the islands in which he referred to them as "Our dear Channel Islanders"

The Liberation Force commenced embarkation in Plymouth on the 9th May and sailed at 16.00 hours on the 11th May, the huge convoy of ships escorted by destroyers sailed to the islands of Jersey and Guernsey. It was a magical sight, as LSTs and transports slipped away from Plymouth on a beautiful evening in May.

The convoys which carried the main force of 6,000 men arrived off the islands of Jersey and Guernsey at 07.00 hours on the 12th May 1945, and began unloading men and vehicles at 08.00 hours.

The German garrison on the islands had been instructed to move a mile back from the towns of St. Helier and St. Peter Port, and not to interfere with the landing of the British Forces. The plans to land on the beaches had been scrapped. In the end the Liberation had developed into something of an anti-climax for the islanders. There was no storming of the beaches, no last ditch stand by the occupying forces, instead a small detachment of 12 men had landed on the 9th May on the islands of Jersey and Guernsey to a rapturous welcome, to raise the Union Jack on British soil after 5 years of German Occupation.

The plan for the liberation of Jersey called for me to take a detachment to this island whilst my sergeant would proceed to Guernsey with a similar number of men. I had been allotted four Military Policemen who together with six of my own men were to land at H+20 minutes, i.e. 08.20 hours. My orders were to proceed to the "Pomme d'Or" Hotel on the Esplanade which had been the German Naval Headquarters, and to take the German Commandant

Pomme d'Or Hotel, St. Helier, Jersey, German Naval Headquarters.

Where the Germans marched in 1940. The Royal Navy leads the Liberation march past in 1945.

(left) Vice Admiral Friedrich Huffmeiier, Commander of the German Forces in the Channel Islands, surrenders on 12th May 1945. He is seen here leaving his Headquarters at the Crown Hotel, St. Peter Port.

Liberation Scene in St. Peter Port, Guernsey.

The scenes of welcome to the Liberation Force in May 1945.

*An LST squeezes between the North and Albert Piers to unload in the
Inner Harbour, Guernsey, 12th May 1945.*

The same ships that brought the Liberation Troops to the island were used to transport the German POWs to the UK. A scene reminiscent of Dunkirk.

(Kapitan Von Kleve) as a prisoner of war. The four Military Policemen were to escort him back to a landing craft en route to England. The Commandant asked for an escort of equal rank, to which I replied that this was not possible and so insisted that he proceed with the escort provided.

My men then started the task of checking the hotel for booby traps, mines etc. Once we had established that the hotel was clear of all devices a signal was sent to Colonel Robinson, who came ashore at 09.55 hours and established his headquarters in the hotel.

The rest of my men together with our vehicles and stores had been scheduled to come ashore during the afternoon, so my second task was to find suitable billets for all of us. I found a hotel in its own grounds to the rear of the town in St. Helier which had previously been used by German troops, this was ideal as it provided parking for my transport. Having ascertained the suitabilty of this accommodation, I was about to go back into St. Helier when a mother with her young daughter approached me, she gave the child a half bottle of brandy which she told me she had kept throughout the occupation for the sole purpose of being able to welcome the first British troops to liberate the island. Unfortunately the little girl in her excitement dropped the bottle before it was handed to me. The tears which followed were however stemmed when we gave her some chocolates and sweets.

On the first few days on Jersey I carried out a reconnaissance around the island, noting the position of minefields, gun emplacements etc. On this reconnaissance it was very noticeable how certain of the islanders were behaving towards their fellow islanders. A great number of houses had been daubed with "Swastikas". I found out later this had been done to denote alleged collaborators and also the many women who had formed associations with the Germans. On our first night in St. Helier the troops had to be called out to break up disturbances in the harbour area, where a gang of men had stripped a number of women, had shaved their heads, tarred and feathered them before throwing them into the water. We also received on this first night a signal warning us of the high incidence of venereal disease which was prevalent on the island and all troops had to be alerted to this grave situation.

We were informed that the Germans had stored large quantities of gelignite at Fort Regent, and this explosive was in a very unstable condition, the Nitro-Glycerine was seeping out of it. We transported this explosive in small quantities in our 3 ton trucks in which we had placed two layers of filled sandbags over the floor area. It was taken to the golf course, where we disposed of it by burning. Many of my men complained of severe headaches through handling this explosive.

After sixteen days on Jersey this detachment sailed for Guernsey, and on arrival made our way to Montville Road, Les Vardes, where the detachment which had landed on the 12th May had made their billets. The platoon was again complete and up to full strength of 42 NCOs and Sappers. We utilised three large detached houses, the one on the corner of Montville Road and Havelands Road became Unit Headquarters.

Immediately after Liberation Day, work got underway in clearing all the minefields, mile upon mile of barbed wire, under-water obstacles etc, etc. Slipways to the beaches which had been sealed off by the Germans were opened up to allow local fishermen access so that they could follow their occupation. Houses and hotels had to be repaired ready for the return of the islanders who had been evacuated in 1940. Reinforced concrete bunkers on the piers at St. Peter Port and St. Sampson's had to be demolished.

On the morning of 29th May 1945 I took over the responsibility for minefield clearance, a meeting had been arranged between myself and the German Engineer Officer (Hauptman Kias) who had during the occupation laid down all the minefields on the island. He brought with him a German Corporal (Obergefreiter Adt) who was to act as interpreter between us for the next 12 months. It had been arranged that 300 POWs from the German Engineer Unit would be retained on the island to carry out minefield clearance, demolitions etc, under the supervision of British Sappers from No. 24 Bomb Disposal Platoon. The Wayside Cheer Hotel at Grandes Rocques had been requisitioned as a POW camp for German Officers and NCOs who had been retained on the island to work on minefield clearance and rehabilitation work. The Germans designated the roads on the island as either RED (Rote) or YELLOW (Gelb). Those running North to South were RED and those running East to West were YELLOW. This made map reading easy. Hauptman Kias would leave the POW camp each morning and rendezvous with me at a pre-arranged point, i.e. where the red road 3, intersected the yellow road 5.

Detailed plans of the minefields were made available to me by Hauptman Kias. Before starting work in a minefield, Kias and I would lay out the base line for each sector of the field. The men would then begin the work of clearance which followed the following pattern. On locating a mine, a safety pin was inserted into the fuse or igniter. The mine was then taken to the end of the field where the igniter was removed and placed in one pile whilst the mine went into another pile. At the end of each working day the mines and igniters were checked against the plans before being transported to the quarry dump. Before the minefield was certified clear and the perimeter barbed wire removed there was one further task to perform which consisted of check sweeping the whole area with mine detectors.

Working 12 hours a day for 7 days a week, with an average of 1,500 mines lifted daily, the work was completed by the 25th July 1945. Working at such a pace it was inevitable that there would be casualties. 6 German POWs lost their lives and 14 were wounded, some seriously. A total of 66,456 mines were lifted.

On the 12th July, I commenced minefield clearance at Baie de Port Grat, (Field No. 108.) which consisted of 392 Tellermines and 467 French anti-tank mines all of which had been fitted with an anti-handling device beneath them. To attempt to lift these mines would have incurred a great loss of life, so I decided that each mine would have to be detonated separately, a slow process but a sensible one. Having evacuated the area I laid a small charge on the first mine

TOTAL NUMBER OF MINES LAID BY TYPE

Year	"S" Mines	Schu Mines	Stock Mines	Booty	Improvised	Tellermines
1940	124					
1941	3393					8
1942	922				518	446
1943	3904				10,519	512
1944	9886	16,924	801	5834	6172	4225
1945	78					
TOTAL	26,607	16,924	801	5834	17,209	5191

TOTAL MINES LAID -	72,566
Mines lifted by German Forces -	6110
Balance to be cleared -	66,456

Note:- "Booty" refers to captured mines ie. British and French.

and covered it with sandbags to deaden the blast. I then retired to a safety point where I had set up the exploder. When I pushed the plunger down there was a terrific explosion which in turn created a shock wave which caused sympathetic detonation across the whole minefield. This blast caused considerable damage to a cottage on the roadside in which a Mrs Duquemin lived. When I met her to explain what had happened, her reply was "Don't worry, you have got rid of the Germans, now the mines, so we can now re-build our lives and live in peace".

The King and Queen were to visit the island on the 7th June 1945, so I received instructions to check the car they would be travelling in for any explosive devices, and to mount a guard on the vehicle at the airport until the arrival of their Royal Highnesses. The men enjoyed a day off work so that they could line the route of the Royal procession.

Whilst minefield clearance was being undertaken, the removal of the anti-landing devices on the beaches, the majority of which had an anti-tank mine attached was undertaken. 300 civilians were recruited and employed in clearing all the anti-landing poles after

Captain H.W. Beckingham RE. with Hauptman Kias, OC319 Engineer Battalion, together with Ober Gefrieter Adt, who acted as our interpreter. Photograph taken behind the Perimeter fence in a Minefield.

Driver/batman Scrivener with Hauptman Kias, OC319 Engineer Battalion, together with Ober Gefrieter Adt, who acted as our interpreter. Photograph taken behind the Perimeter fence in a Minefield.

(left) German POWs clearing "Schu Mines" around the airfield perimeter.

Igniters being removed from "Schu Mines"

my men had removed the explosive charges. They were also responsible for the clearance of many miles of barbed wire which covered large areas of the island. By the beginning of August we turned our attentions to clearing the 1,000 Roll Bombs which had been suspended from the cliff tops on the South coast. Many of these had to be blown in-situ. Warning notices were published in the local press which asked people living in the vicinity to open all their windows to minimise damage from possible blast. Unfortunately there were a few unscruplous people who tried to capitalise from this operation, we received claims for compensation for damage caused to greenhouses which were located many miles away from the detonation and could not possibly have been affected.

At the beginning of August there still remained the under water obstacles situated in Fermain Bay, Petit Bot Bay and Saints Bay. These consisted of steel girders sunk into the sand which were attached by wires to a 300 lb. French Shell. These obstacles were below water even at Spring tides, and to add to the problem, I was informed that the main telephone cable between Jersey and Guernsey entered the sea at Saints Bay and under no circumstances could these obstacles be removed by detonation. I decided that the only way of dealing with these obstacles would be for me to don a diving suit to enable me to stay under water long enough to render these shells safe prior to their removal. I therefore asked the naval authorities in Portsmouth if I could borrow a self contained diving suit and all the necessary equiptment. Once this had arrived on the island, the next step was to wait for a suitable Spring tide so that I would be working in a minimum depth of water. On 13th and 14th August 1945 I set about the task in Fermain Bay and the whole operation went without an hitch. Having gained my confidence as a diver I decided to tackle the obstacles in Saints Bay but would have to wait for the next Spring tide which would occur on 22nd and 23rd September. I started work at low water and had cleared four obstacles and was about to start on the fifth when a wave suddenly rocked me off my feet, I instinctively made a grab for the girder when a POW standing alongside me shouted "Nein, Oberleutnant!" He not only saved my life but also his own. Possibly it was the latter that was more important to him. No further unforseen incidents took place and Saints Bay was cleared of all its deadly impediments. I often wonder whether the thousands of holiday makers who sit and swim off the beach in the bay each Summer realise what the bay and the surrounding area looked like in 1945.

Chapter Six

The joy of Liberation lasted for a very short time. During the first few days on the island the British troops marched the German POWs down to the beach and supervised their loading onto the landing craft that had brought us to the island. Girl friends of the German troops watched, many trying to get close to their German lovers. During this period many islanders had raided German billets and installations and stolen binoculars, pistols, uniforms, medals etc as souvenirs. Within 24 hours of the Germans evacuating their gun batteries, bunkers and their billets the islanders had plundered these and had stolen virtually everything of value.

30,000 German troops were transported to POW camps in England whilst a number were retained to assist in the rehabilition process.

It was only after the Liberation that women who had solaced themselves with German lovers faced condemnation, hatred and resentment against those who had fraternised suddenly erupted, they were christened "Jerrybags".

Stealing was looked upon as a legitimate occupation by many of the islanders. One of our vehicles was deprived of its four wheels in the lorry park in spite of patrolling sentries, on another occasion a 24 hour ration pack was taken from outside our cook house in broad daylight.

During my travels around the island from one minefield to another I happened to call on a large house situated in the parish of St Martins and on gaining access found to my surprise I had walked into a German brothel. There were a number of French girls present. I reported this to headquarters, but do not recall the final outcome. Also during this period it was common practice to receive "tip offs" that certain of the islanders were harbouring Germans who had discarded their uniforms. I came across one such case in the parish of St. Saviour late in August.

Transporting the POWs from the prison camp to the work sites created a problem, for on many occasions we had screaming girls running after the trucks trying to throw letters to the prisoners.

Towards the end of 1945 those islanders who had been evacuated, together with those who had served in the forces, started to return to their homes. They were incensed to find their houses had been looted and the majority of the islanders who had remained behind in 1940 had secured themselves lucrative jobs.

They also found in many cases that their wives and sisters had conceived illegitimate children fathered by the German troops. Government sources reveal that many hundreds of local women, including those whose husbands were away fighting for Britain were sleeping with the enemy. Altogether many hundreds of German offsprings were born before the end of the occupation, with many more on the way. Abortions, although illegal on the islands, were innumerable. Inevitably, the subject of collaborators and informers was to be raised by the islanders, they knew of many cases and were anxious to see justice done. A number of accusations were submitted, but it was agreed with the Home Office that no action be taken in regards to women who had associated with the Germans or people who had entertained them as their guests. After five years of war the British Government did not wish to pursue any claims and were only too anxious to draw a veil over the whole problem of collaboration. This resulted in a number of collaborators and informers going free without any charges being brought against them for their previous actions. In December 1945 the Bailiff, Victor Carey received a knighthood and the President of the Controlling Committeee, Major A.J. Sherwill received a CBE. There were many on the island who felt that they should have stood trial as collaborators. So political prudence won the day.

When the German Luftwaffe bombed St. Peter Port on Friday 28th June 1940 they dropped three 250 kg. Bombs in the area of La Capelles which failed to explode. These three UXBs lay silent and lethal for over five years. The holes of entry were discovered on the site of some dilapidated greenhouses. The work of recovering these bombs was undertaken by German POWs working under the supervision of British sappers from No.24 Bomb Disposal Platoon RE. I defused these bombs without incident, even though one of them had a (17) delayed action clockwork fuse fitted.

The Germans had a major Radar installation sited within the confines of Fort George, and prior to "D" Day the allied airforce paid particular attention to it. On the 27th May 1944, 24 Typhoons attacked this installation to put it out of action prior to the landings in Normandy on the 6th June 1944. Many properties in the vicinity were damaged during this raid. On the 4th June 1945 whilst clearing a minefield situated on the cliff tops overlooking Soldiers Bay we uncovered a British 500 lb bomb which had been dropped by the Canadian Air-force during the raid on Fort George and had failed to explode on impact. We defused this bomb before continuing to clear the minefield.

In the 1990s the Gas Board were laying new gas mains in the Fort Road area when they uncovered a UXB which had been dropped during this raid. It had lain undetected for more than 46 years.

The island had been under military rule from Liberation Day until the 25th August 1945, when the responsibilities were transferred to the Civil Administration. To mark the departure of Force 135 from the island the Governor arranged a Ball at Government House for all the Officers in the force. I had received my invitation from Colonel Wilkinson, but when I said to him that I would have to refuse on the grounds that I did not know any member of the opposite sex on the island, his answer to me was "well you are going to attend so I suggest you find yourself a partner". My problem was solved when one day I saw my sergeant talking to an attractive girl in St. Peter Port. When I questioned him as to who the young lady was, he said he had seen her on a few occasions when on his travels, and had stopped to pass the time of day with her. I asked if he knew where she lived and was told in the Hautville next to the house where Victor Hugo used to reside. I took it upon myself to visit the house where I met her mother to whom I explained my predicament. She said her daughter would be delighted to accompany me to the Ball, so on the night of the Ball my batman drove us both to Government House. We spent a very enjoyable evening, the dancing went on into the early hours of the moming and we finally departed at 3.00am. Following our first meeting the two of us would steal ourselves away on many warm and sunny afternoons and spend our time swimming off the many beaches on the South coast of the island. After the traumas of the last few years we were becoming "civilised" once again and enjoying the youth we had missed out on over the previous five years of war. Unfortunately for me this young lady took up an appointment in London shortly afterwards.

At the end of August the only units left were the Royal Engineers who were working on the rehabilitation of houses and hotels and my unit who were busy destroying gun emplacements, bunkers etc. A small detachment of Infantry who were acting as guards at the POW camp were also retained.

In September 1945, No.125 Works Section RE commenced the building of a camp using "Nissen" huts, on a piece of land at Fort George which overlooked the Fort Road. The Engineer units moved into this accommodation at the end of October, thus freeing a number of properties which in turn would cater for the islanders, who by this time were beginning to return home. Having settled into our new camp, the work of clearing the island of all German fortifications and the rehabilitation work to hotels etc, continued, although at a more leisurely pace. Unfortunately several private residences and hotels were destroyed during the occupation because they interfered with the "field of fire" of the heavy gun batteries, others were demolished to allow fortifications to be built on their site. Two prominent landmarks were destroyed; the "De Saumarez Memorial" in Delancy Park and the "Doyle Column" at Jerbourg.

One of the first hotels to be rehabitated and re-opened was the "Beaulieu" at St. Martins (now renamed the Carlton). This became the favourite watering hole for the Engineer troops. It was not long before dances were being organised on a number of evenings each week. On one of my visits to this hostelry I met a young lady who had just returned to the island having spent the occupation years in Bournemouth. We became close friends and on many social occasions she joined me in our Mess and took part in our dances and games evenings. I learned that whilst in Bournemouth she had married a Canadian Air Force Pilot who in the December of 1945, came over to the island on leave, the three of us made a very happy threesome and spent much time in each other's company visiting the hostelries on the island. On my return to the island in 1988, I set out to find them but was told that after the war they had emigrated to Canada and had not made any return trips to the island.

The Germans had built a massive reinforced concrete bunker on the end of White Rock pier which was taking some time to demolish as the walls were 6-00 ft thick. A working party on site each day drilled a series of holes in the concrete and these were filled with explosives. Detonators were fixed to the charges and wired to an exploder sited at a safety point. It had been arranged that any ship lying alongside the quay would put to sea at 16.00 hours each day when I would arrive on site and take charge of the demolition by detonating the charges. One day we had a problem, as when I pushed the plunger of the exploder, "nothing happened". I waited and waited before approaching the bunker. Then my mind was made up for me when I noticed a ship steaming towards the harbour entrance. There was only one course of action for me to take. I rushed along the quay and started pulling the detonators out of the charges. I was lucky and got away with it.

In November 1945, I was invited to take lunch with the Rotary Club at the Royal Hotel, in St. Peter Port, and after lunch I was introduced to a Mr C.R. Falla who told me he lived at "La Trigale" in the Forest, and hoped I could solve a problem for him. At the start of the occupation he had buried some rare Sheffield plate and silverware and other precious items, but after five years of occupation could not now remember where he had buried this treasure. I went along to Mr Falla's house armed with a mine detector and after sweeping an area of his garden I found his treasure untouched and no worse for its long period in "hiding". Towards the end of 1945 islanders were returning in large numbers and were amazed at the picture which met their eyes. They had left a peaceful and tranquil island in 1940, and had come back to an impregnable fortress. Many found the joy of returning home saddened on finding that their wives and sisters had conceived illegitimate children fathered by German troops.

With the island being opened up, many of the civilians took to walking on the beaches and we had numerous reports of Tellermines which had been washed off the beach defences being found. All these isolated incidents were successfully dealt with. One day the police reported to me that a civilian whilst walking on the beach had accidently stepped onto a Tellermine, and his injuries were such that he had been taken to hospital. I decided to visit this man to ascertain his injuries, and was surprised to find that he had shrapnel wounds to his body, but there were no injuries to his legs. If he had trodden on a mine then he would most certainly have lost his legs. I had the unpleasant task of telling this person that I did not believe his story, and suggested to him that the most likely story was that he had found this mine lying on the rocks and he had been throwing stones at it, and to his great surprise he had detonated it. Unfortunately he was not the only civilian to make up a story in the hopes of claiming compensation.

In February 1946 we held a mess night to which we had invited members of the Sergeant's Mess to join us, they in turn brought along with them a number of lady guests. It turned out to be quite a party. Two of the girls had recently returned to the island after serving with ENSA as singers and had spent their war years in England entertaining the troops. They entertained us by putting on their cabaret act in which they sang a selection of songs from the current Ivor Novello musical "Perchance to Dream". They asked that I should join them in singing my favourite song from that show which was "We'll gather lilacs in the Spring again", as my voice bears no resemblance to Sinatra's or Crosby's it became quite hilarious.

I thought nothing more about this evening until about a week or so later a Staff Sergeant who had been at our party came to see me with an invitation to join himself and one or two others at a party the two girls were hosting. Needless to say I went along and, having spent a very pleasant evening, found myself arranging to meet one of the girls later in the week. This one particular girl became a very close friend. I would escort both of them to the various venues where they were performing around the island, so my last few months on the island were spent in very charming and delightful company.

This particular young lady came over to England in the Summer of 1946 to appear in a Summer show at "The De La Warr" Pavilion in Bexhill. After which we lost touch with each other until in 1990, my wife and I on a visit to Guernsey were told she had returned to the island and we were given her address. We decided to call on her, and as I knocked on her door my wife said "I hope she doesn't have a weak heart, because the shock of meeting you after over forty years could be too much for her to cope with." It was most interesting to note that after all those years she immediately recognised me. We spent a very pleasant and informative afternoon reliving old times of yester year, and going over old photographs. From that day on we kept in touch until her death in 1994.

On the 2nd April 1946 I received a message from a Mr Prior, who was the caretaker on the small island of Herm, that a large object had been washed ashore on Shell Beach. I collected four of my men and sailed over to the island, which lies about 3 miles off

Guernsey. On reaching the beach I recognised the "object" as a 1,000 lb Aerial Torpedo. A gun-cotton charge was prepared and placed on the casing and, after retiring to a safe distance, I detonated the charge.

Almost as if in salute an RAF plane circled Herm twice and in doing a final straight run, dipped its wings over the party on the beach. The shattered casing was rolled down the beach and into the sea where it would rest in the same "graveyard" as the tide-washed remains of an RAF fighter plane which was brought down between 1940 and 1945. The Germans had removed the engine from this plane leaving only the framework which is now overgrown with seaweed and exposed to the air at very low tides.

On our return journey to Guernsey we still had with us a number of 2 oz, gun cotton primers, detonators and safety fuse, so we resorted to a spot of easy fishing. Our catch was incredible, both of fish and eels, we collected two buckets full of prime fish, one was given to the fisherman who had taken us over to Herm, and who had come up with the idea that we should catch a few fish on our return journey, the other load went into the Officer's Mess. There were so many fish, that to keep them until required, we filled a bath in our ablution block which acted as a fish tank.

On the 24th April 1946, I received three reports of anti-ship mines having been washed ashore, one was in the vicinity of the Martello tower at Vazon Bay, one close to Fort Saumarez and the third at Grande Rocque, this latter mine turned out to be a German Type GY*, the other two were both British, Type Mk. XVII.

Although over the previous six years I had dealt with hundreds of unexploded bombs, thousands of landmines, shells etc, this was the first time I had seen a real anti-ship mine, bristling with "horns" on its casing. I approached these three deadly killers with some trepidation, as I was hoping to leave the island in June and did not want to be blown sky high at this late stage in my career.

The first mine I tackled was the British one which had been found on the beach in Vazon Bay. On arrival at the beach I emptied my pockets, took off my watch, then my boots and handed these to my sergeant and told him to go back to my PU truck and wait there for me. I had endeavoured to approach the mine with no metal objects on my person just in case it had a magnetic fuse installed. It was very lonely on that beach as I started the task of defusing this mine. I began by unscrewing the plate at the base of the mine which gave me access to all the electrical circuits, and then proceeded to cut these wires, one by one. The relief I felt was overwhelming when I realised I had cut all the wires and I was still in one piece. As mentioned previously, the greatest danger a Bomb Disposal Officer faced was over confidence, one had always to practice patience and treat all explosive devices with respect. This was the secret to a reasonably long life.

I then moved along the coast to Fort Saumarez and found this mine to be of German origin, this was defused successfully, using similar methods as those adopted for the British mine. Then I travelled up to Grande Rocque where the third mine to come ashore was found, this again was of German origin. This mine proved difficult to deal with because it was floating in a depth of water which meant I had to wade waist deep to get close enough to work on it, however the mission was accomplished and all the mines had been rendered safe. The three mines were collected by my men and taken to Chouet Quarry where they were detonated.

The following morning I was summoned to Government House where I was greeted by the Lieut. Governor of the island, Lieut. General Sir Phillip Neame, VC. with the words "Glad I didn't have to buy you a wreath yesterday". It was perhaps the perfect ending, having served seven years in HM Forces throughout the War to finish my service on British soil. In 1939, I and my two colleagues had been called up on the 1st September and within a few months we had been separated, my two friends went out to the Middle East whilst I spent the whole of the war years in England. My first overseas posting came on the 9th May 1945, when I sailed with the Liberation Force to the Channel Islands.

Having spent twelve months in Guernsey destroying German fortifications and generally tidying up the island ready for the returning islanders, and later the holidaymakers on whom much of the islands economy depended; the time came for me to say farewell to this beautiful and idyllic island.

Over the years researchers and journalists have written many books on the occupation of the Channel Islands, many experiences have been related, some true, but many have been embellished to such a degree that they have become the product of a vivid imagination. I quote one instance only, but there are many more on record to show how the imagination has been allowed to run riot. A Jersey boy tells of going onto the cliff tops and defusing mines. Some mines he states were magnetic. As the Bomb Disposal Officer responsible for the clearance of all the minefields on Guernsey I can assure the reader that there were no magnetic mines used in the Channel Islands. Such stories, however, make good copy when talking to researchers etc.

At the end of April 1946 the German POWs who had worked hard and diligently over the proceeding ten months alongside my men in clearing the island of all the minefields, Roll bombs, underwater obstacles etc, were to leave for POW camps in England. At our final meeting, Hauptman Kias presented me with his map case, saying he would have no further use for it. Also at this meeting a POW who before the war had been a wood carver in Bavaria presented me with a wooden plaque on which he had carved the badge of the "Royal Engineers". Producing this had occupied his evenings in the POW camp. This was a fitting memento, which I have treasured over the years.

In March 1946 my sergeant who had come to Guernsey with the Liberation Force returned to England for demobilisation and his replacement was none other than one of my friends who had enlisted with me and whom I had not seen since 1940. What an amazing coincidence, of all the thousands of troops around the world they had selected my friend as a replacement. What a small world!

In the 1970s Fort George and its battlements were demolished and the land cleared, in its place has been built an estate of expensive houses which have been bought by wealthy incomers looking for a tax haven. This development angered many of the local and true islanders who would have preferred to see a development of low cost housing, but high investment and finance won the day.

In 1995, the island celebrated the 50th anniversary of their Liberation, a commemoration medal was presented to a small number of the members of Force 135 whom the States of Guernsey had managed to find after such a lapse of time. During these celebrations I had the honour of being presented to HRH The Prince of Wales by the Bailiff, Sir Graham Dorey. During our conversation the prince asked what the motif on my tie represented. This was the bomb disposal badge which I was able to tell him had been designed by his Great Grandmother (Queen Mary) in 1940. He showed great interest in this snippet of information.

During 1960 it became clear that the emphasis in Bomb Disposal was changing from the disposal of conventional towards the disposal of guided weapons. The time had come to commemorate in some way the gallantry of all ranks of the Corps of Royal Engineers, who had distinguished themselves in this exceptionally hazardous and unpleasant form of warfare - the disposal of the unexploded bomb, more commonly referred to as the UXB.

The UXB was a menace which had never been imagined prior to 1940. It might be unexploded by deliberate design of the enemy or by accident. Either way it was a hazard to morale, life and property and had to be removed. Because the bombs buried themselves deep in the earth, under foundations, by railways, in factory floors and similar difficult places, only the Royal Engineers had the combination of Civil, Mechanical and Explosive engineering knowledge to deal with them.

The cost was high, 246 Officers and men lost their lives and to this must be added another 151 who were killed clearing our own minefields. Twelve George Crosses and countless other decorations were earned. The casualty ratio was two killed to one wounded.